Before each trip, the members sit together and propose necessary dishes in order to make adequate cuisine to fulfill everyone's preferences. However, because picnics and camping activities are usually done in a short period of time, such as 1-2 days, the dishes and take-out food must meet the criteria of being simple, quick, and compact, as well as being able to be stored for a long time. People have more time to travel, converse, and plan group activities.

Aside from determining the site and appropriate camping equipment for a fun and safe picnic with your family or group of friends over the weekend, take-out food is also very significant. It is worthwhile to pay attention.

So, what should you bring on a picnic or camping trip? Let's have a look at the list of simple, easy-to-make, and easy-to-carry camping and picnic foods developed from the material of the book we're bringing today

4

CONTENTS

French Toast Sticks 8

Frittata 11

Grilled Halloumi Sandwich 14

French Toast 17

Cinnamon Apple Pancakes 19

Dutch Oven Enchiladas 22

Jalapeño Popper Dogs 25

Lentil Sloppy Joes 27

Foil Pack Chicken Nachos 32

Grilled Corn on the Cob 34

Berry Crisp Foil Packs 36

Cilantro-Lime Shrimp Foil Packs 38

Campfire French Toast 40

Burger 42

Campfire Popcorn 45

Grilled Cheese Dogs 47

Grilled Pizza Bread 49

Grilled Asparagus 51

Grilled Summer Fruit Skewers 53

Hot Shot Grilled Salmon	55
S'mores Cinnamon Rolls	57
Grilled Pork Chops	59
Sausage and Peppers Foil Pack	61
Grilled Watermelon	63
Chicken Fajitas	65
Goulash	67
Cheesy Taco Skillet	70
Grilled Steak Skewers with Chimichurri	72
Party Shrimp Boil	75
Chicken and Black Bean Nachos	78
Skillet Spinach-Artichoke Dip	81
Tofu, Tomato, and Zucchini Kebabs	84
Beer-Braised Chicken	86
Seared Sausage with Cabbage	89
Grilled Corn with Red Pepper Jelly Glaze	92
Marinated Chicken and Onion Kebabs	94
Blackberry-Glazed Chicken	97
Chicken and Sweet Potato Kebabs	99
Apple Seed Oatmeal	101
Brats with Peppers and Onions	103
Stove Chilaquiles	105

Shakshuka	108
Banana Coconut French Toast	111
CHEESY GARLIC FRIES IN FOIL	114
Campfire Queso	117
Chicken Pasta Salad	119
Breakfast Foil Packs	122
Cajun Shrimp Kebabs	124
Campfire Cinnamon Rolls	126
Grilled Chicago Dogs	127
Campfire Nachos	129
Tzatziki Chicken Skewers	131
Chickpea Curry	134
Dutch Oven Mac & Cheese	137
Foil Wrapped Baked Sweet Potatoes and Chili	139
Chicken Pineapple Kabobs	142
Pie Pizza Pockets	145
Camp Chilaquiles	148

French Toast Sticks

Element

- 4 slices of Texas toast, or other thick slices of bread
- 2 eggs
- 1/2 cup of milk
- 1 teaspoon sugar
- 1 teaspoon cinnamon
- A little salt

- 2 tablespoons butter
- Berry and maple syrup to serve

Guide

Cut the bread into 1½ inch long sticks.

Beat two eggs until they are completely combined. Add milk, sugar, cinnamon and a little salt. Mix.

Heat a tablespoon of butter over medium heat in a non-stick pan.

Soak the toast in a mixture of eggs and milk, soak the toast in the liquid for a few seconds, then turn it over and soak the other side for a few seconds.

Lift the mixture out of the mixture and let it drip extra. Put it in a pot. Repeat with another toast stick. You can fit about half of the sticks in a 10-inch or 12-inch pot.

When one side of the toast turns golden (about 3 minutes), turn the other side over and bake for about 2 minutes.

Remove it and set it aside
.

Heat a second spoon of butter and repeat the process until all toast sticks are complete.

Soak fresh berries on the sides with maple syrup. interesting!

Frittata

Element

- 8 eggs
- 1/2 cup of milk
- 1/2 teaspoon sea salt
- 1/4 teaspoon of freshly ground pepper

- 2 tablespoons of olive oil, split
- 1 thinly sliced shallot
- Cherry tomato 1 pint, half
- ¼ basil, chopped
- Shred Gruyere cheese ½ cup

Guide

Prepare a campfire or charcoal for cooking.

In a medium bowl, whisk until egg, milk, salt and pepper are mixed. Save it.

Heat 1 tablespoon of oil in a 10 inch frying pan over medium heat. Add shallot and fry for 7-10 minutes until tender and brown.

Raise the campfire or move the pot to the cold side of the grill to reduce medium to low heat. Put the tomatoes in a pan, then add the mixture of eggs, basil and cheese. Put the lid on. Spread the embers over the entire lid.

Cook for about 15 minutes until the frittata swells and the eggs just harden (check in 10 minutes to measure progress and open the lid with heat-resistant gloves or a lid lifter).

Enjoy with additional cheese and basil if needed!

Grilled Halloumi Sandwich

Material

- 1 large Hawaiian sweet roll (use sandwich if found)
- 1 tablespoon butter or oil, cup
- 2 ounces Harumi cheese, slices
- 1 egg
- 3 tablespoons mayo

- 1 tablespoon Sriracha, (more or less depending on your heat preference)
- 1 green onion sliced or minced
- Salt and pepper, season to taste

Guide

Toast the pan bread on a frying pan or bake. Save it.

Heat half of the butter or oil in a saucepan over medium heat. When it's melted, add the cheese. Fry on both sides for about 3-4 minutes each until the spots turn golden. Save it.

This step can also be done on the grill. In that case, skip the butter/oil and place the cheese directly on the griddle.

Heat remaining butter or oil over medium heat. Once melted, crack the eggs into the frying pan. Completely optional step: Once the whites start to set, you can use a fork to mix some of the yolks and spread some over the yolks. This will produce egg yolks for each bite.

Cook eggs for about 4 minutes or until eggs are cooked to your liking.

Prepare the spicy mayonnaise while the eggs are being cooked. In a small bowl (or measuring cup), mix mayonnaise and Sriracha.

To combine, spread spicy mayonnaise on each cut surface of the bread. Enjoy grilled Halloumi, eggs, scallions and salt and pepper.

French Toast

Element

- 1 loaf of bread
- 3 eggs
- 1 cup of milk
- 2 tablespoons of sugar, sprinkle more

- 1 teaspoon cinnamon
- 1 teaspoon vanilla extract, optional
- 1/4 teaspoon nutmeg, optional
- 4 tablespoons of butter for bread
- Maple syrup and berries on top

Guide

Cut the bread to a thickness of 3/4 "-1".

First, break the egg into a bowl large enough to hold a slice of bread. Then add milk, cinnamon, nutmeg, vanilla and sugar until well mixed. Heat 4 tablespoons of butter in a saucepan over medium heat.

Soak the sliced bread in a mixture of eggs and milk and place on both sides for about 10 seconds. To dissolve the excess, sprinkle sugar on both sides and fry in a frying pan for about 3 minutes until golden and crispy.

Repeat with the remaining bread and add butter to the pan as needed.

Serve with maple syrup, fresh fruit and hot coffee. exciting!

Cinnamon Apple Pancakes

Material

- 1 egg
- Whole milk ½ cup
- ½ cup cider with seasoning
- 1 tablespoon melted butter
- 1 cup flour
- 2 spoons of sugar

- 1 teaspoon baking powder
- 1/2 teaspoon salt
- ½ cup chopped apples
- Grease a pan with butter or oil
- Maple syrup
- Cinnamon apple topping
- 1 apple sliced or chopped
- 1 tablespoon butter
- 1 teaspoon sugar
- 1 teaspoon cinnamon

Guide

To make butter, place eggs, milk, cider, and melted butter in a medium bowl with a whisk. Add flour, sugar, baking powder and salt, stir well. Add chopped apples.

Heat a skillet or iron plate over medium heat. Grease the surface thoroughly, then pour in ¼ cup of flour at a time.

When the underside of the cake turns golden and begins to form small bubbles on the top, flip the cake over and cook until golden. Repeat with the rest of the dough.

To make the cinnamon apple topping, melt 1 tablespoon butter in a saucepan and add sliced apples, sugar, and cinnamon. Toss to coat the apples evenly and sauté for a few minutes until apples are tender.

Enjoy pancakes with cinnamon apple and maple syrup.

Dutch Oven Enchiladas

Material

- 2 tablespoons of oil
- Cut a red bell pepper into strips
- Purple onion cut into half thin slices
- 4 minced garlic
- 1 tablespoon dill

- 2 teaspoons salt
- Enchilada sauce 14 oz
- 2 cups cheese
- 1 cup cooked black beans
- 4-6 flour cakes
- Present
- Coriander, jalapeno, lemon, etc.

Guide

Prepare charcoal or make a campfire so you can cook with embers.

Heat oil in Dutch oven over medium heat. Add pepper and fry for a few minutes until soft. Add onion and sauté until onion is soft, translucent and peppers are cooked through.

Add garlic, cumin and salt and fry for 30 seconds until fragrant. Remove from heat and transfer vegetables to a plate or bowl.

Add 1/2 cup of enchilada sauce to coat the bottom of the Dutch oven.
To make the enchilada, place the onion and peppers in the center of the flour tortillas. Add a spoonful of black beans

and top with cheese. Roll the tortillas around the filling and place the enchilada in the Dutch oven with the seam facing down. Repeat with remaining ingredients. This recipe makes 4-6 enchiladas, depending on the size of the Dutch oven.

Coat the remaining sauce and cheese over the enchilada. Place the lid on top.

Return the Dutch oven to the campfire. Place it over indirect heat (campfire grills work well) and stack 14-16 coals on the lid. Cook for about 10 minutes until cheese is melted.

Serve with jalapeno peppers, coriander and lemon wedge on top.

Jalapeño Popper Dogs

Element

- 12 oversized jalapenos
- 8 slices of American cheese
- 4 thin sausages, half the length
- 4 sausage rolls
- Mustard, offer

Direction

High baking temperature. Cut off the top of the jalapeno and the bottom of the part that begins to narrow. Use a knife to remove the stems and veins of each pepper to form a hollow tube.

Crush the cheese into a rectangle about the same width as the sausage. Place a few on half of the sausage, then place the other half of the dog on top and put the cheese in the center to change the shape of the sausage.

Push the sausage into the jalapeno tube. (You can place two or three around each sausage, depending on the size of the jalapeno.)

Grill and bake jalapenos in all directions to warm the dog, but turn off the heat before the cheese spills. Serve with hot dogs with mustard.

Lentil Sloppy Joes

Element

- 1/2 tablespoon of oil
- 1 onion, diced
- 1 Anaheim pepper, diced
- 2 tablespoons of tomato paste

- 3 pieces of chopped garlic
- ½ cup red lentils
- 1 cup of water or soup
- 1 teaspoon mustard
- 1 tablespoon maple syrup
- 2 teaspoons of apple cider vinegar
- 1 teaspoon vegan Worcestershire
- 1 teaspoon chili powder
- Salt spoon
- service
- 2 cakes

Guide

Heat the oil over medium heat and add chopped onions and Anaheim pepper. Fry for about 3-4 minutes until the onions are tender and start to turn golden. Add ketchup and fry for 1 minute, add garlic and fry for 1 minute.

Add red lentils and 1½ cups of water to the saucepan. Bring to a boil and then reduce the heat. Cook for 10 to 15 minutes with occasional stirring until the lentils are fairly tender but not muddy.

Add mustard, maple syrup, apple cider vinegar, Worcestershire vinegar, chili powder and salt. Mix. Boil for 3-5 minutes until the sauce is a little thicker.

Serve cupcakes with your favorite toppings and sides!

Skillet Beer Cheese

Material
- 3c. Chopped Cheddar
- 1 (8 oz block) cream cheese, soft
- 2 cloves minced garlic
- 1 tbsp. In addition to chopped chives, garnish chives
- 1 C. Alcohol
- Kosher salt
- Cayenne pepper
- Slice of toast to serve

Direction

Place the net over the campfire. In a large cast iron skillet, add cheddar cheese, cream cheese, garlic, chives and beer, season with salt and cayenne pepper. Cover with foil.

Cook over a campfire for about 15 minutes until melted. Served with bread slices.

Foil Pack Chicken Nachos

Element
- 1 bag of tortilla chips
- 2C. Shredded chicken rotisserie
- 1 / 2c. Red enchilada sauce
- 1 (15 ounces) Burnt roasted tomatoes can be chopped and drained
- 1 C. Black beans, drainage
- 1 1 / 2c. Shredded cheddar
- 1 1 / 2c. Chopped Monterey Jack

- Freshly chopped coriander, for garnish (optional)
- Sour cream, provided (optional)

Direction

Heat the grill to medium heat. Put chicken, enchilada sauce, tomatoes and black beans in a large bowl. Divide the tortillas into 4 large foils and top with french fries. Place the cheese on top of each and fold it into individual packets.

Place the package on an iron plate and bake for about 15 minutes until the cheese melts and the chicken mixture is completely heated.

If used, decorate with coriander and sour cream.

Grilled Corn on the Cob

Material
- Corn with four peeled ears
- For butter and serving
- Kosher salt

Direction

Preheat the grill to a high temperature and cook for 10 minutes. (Or preheat the baking pan over high heat.) Add the corn and cook completely for about 10 minutes until everything burns.

Warm the corn with butter and season with salt.

Berry Crisp Foil Packs

Material
- 3c. Mixed strawberries (raspberries, blueberries, blackberries)
- Juice of 1/2 lemon
- 1/4c. Brown sugar, cup
- 2 C. Old fashioned rolled oats
- 1 tbsp. All-purpose flour
- 1/3c. Peaches chopped
- 1/4c. Butter softened and cut into cubes
- 1 teaspoon cinnamon

- 1/2 teaspoon kosher salt
- Vanilla ice cream, to serve

Direction

Heat the grill to high heat. Create four 8x-8 inch foil bags and grease with cooking spray. In a large bowl, mix until blended with berries, lime juice, and 1 tablespoon brown sugar. Save it.

In a separate bowl, mix the oats, flour, pecans, butter, remaining brown sugar, cinnamon, and salt and stir together until a top layer forms.

Place half of the strawberries on top of the foil, then half of the cake mix on top. say again.

Fold the foil bag and seal it.

Bake for 15-20 minutes until the berries are bubbly and the oat mixture is fully cooked.

Let cool a bit then serve with vanilla ice cream.

Cilantro-Lime Shrimp Foil Packs

Element
- 1 pound medium shrimp, peel and sow
- Three ears of corn
- Cut one zucchini in half
- 2 pieces of chopped garlic
- 2 teaspoons. Spoon is the earth

1 teaspoon. Crushed red pepper
- 2 tablespoons. Chopped fresh coriander
- Extra virgin olive oil for drizzle
- Kosher salt
- Freshly ground black pepper
- Cut 2 lemons into round pieces
- 2 tablespoons. butter

Direction

In a large bowl, mix shrimp, corn, zucchini, garlic, cumin, red pepper and coriander. Sprinkle with olive oil, season with salt and pepper, and stir until mixed.

Spread 4 foils. Divide the shrimp mixture into layers of foil and coat each layer with butter and lemon slices. Sealed package.

High baking temperature. Put the shrimp wrap and bake for about 10 minutes until the shrimp turns pink.

Service.

Campfire French Toast

Material

For butter and foil
- 5 big eggs
- 1/4c. whole milk
- 1 tbsp. Granulated sugar
- 1 teaspoon pure vanilla essence
- pinch of kosher salt
- 1 loaf of sliced white bread

- 1 C. Sliced strawberries to serve
- 1/4c. Powdered sugar, for garnish
- Maple syrup, to serve

Direction

Butter a large piece of foil to shape the boat. Stand up to keep the shape of the bread and place a slice of bread inside. (It doesn't matter if the slice opens up a little.) Add another foil underneath for double coverage.

In a large liquid measuring cup, whisk together eggs, milk, sugar, vanilla, and salt with a whisk. Carefully pour into the bread so that it fits snugly between each slice.

Cover the entire loaf with foil. Place over campfire - not on the hottest part - about 40 minutes until egg mixture is fully cooked and bread is lightly toasted.

Let sit for 10 minutes before serving. Sprinkle with powdered sugar and garnish with sliced strawberries. Enjoy warmly with syrup.

Burger

Material
- 1 pound minced beef
- Kosher salt
- Freshly ground black pepper
- 2 tbsp. Melted butter
- 3 slices of cheese like American
- For service
- 3 hamburgers

- 1 large sliced tomato
- Ice lettuce
- Chopped white onion

Direction

Shape the beef into three equal sized patties, about an inch wider than the bread. Season with salt and pepper on both sides of each patty. Push a wide shallow groove into the center of each hamburger.

When grilling: Heat a griddle or baking pan over high heat. Bake the dough for 6 minutes until the crust develops and is no longer pink. Flip and immediately polish with melted butter on each piece of cake. Cook for 3 more minutes and then add the cheese. For medium, continue cooking for 3 more minutes until desired finish is achieved.

When cooking in a pan: Heat a pan over medium to high heat and add the flour and cook for 6 minutes until the crust expands and loses its pink color.

Flip and immediately polish with melted butter on each piece of cake. Cook for 3 more minutes and then add the cheese. For medium, continue cooking for 3 more minutes until desired finish is achieved.

Clamp the hamburger in the center of the pan with the fixing tool of your choice.

Campfire Popcorn

Element
- 1 / 4c. Butter popcorn
- 1 tablespoon. Vegetable oil
- 1/4 teaspoon. garlic powder
- Kosher salT

Direction

Put popcorn seeds and vegetable oil in a cake can. Cover it tightly with foil and put flour on top to leave enough space for the corn to swell and make a campfire.

Use the tongs and shake slowly until the tin pie stops. Season with garlic powder and salt.

Grilled Cheese Dogs

Material
- 4 sausage sandwiches
- 2 tablespoons. Soft butter
- 1/4 teaspoon garlic powder
- 1/4 teaspoon onion powder
- 4 sausages divided vertically (be careful not to cut them completely)

- 3c. Chopped cheddar cheese
- 4 thinly sliced onions

Direction

Flatten the sausage bread with a rolling pin. Mix butter, garlic powder and onion powder in a small bowl. Spread on the outside of the bread.

Bake both sides on medium heat for 2 minutes in a large frying pan until the sausages are browned (make batches as needed). Save it.

Place the cake in a buttered frying pan on the back and add 1/2 cup cheddar cheese, sausage, a little more cheddar cheese, and 1/4 onion on top.

Cook over medium heat until the cheese melts and cover with a spoon. Repeat with the rest of the ingredients to make a total of 4 cheese dogs.

Grilled Pizza Bread

Material
- 1 loaf of big bread, half
- 115 ounces. Pizza sauce
- 3c. Finely chopped mozzarella cheese
- 1 / 3c. Smoke sausage
- 1 / 4c. black olives
- 1/2 purple onion, half slice
- 1 chili pepper, chopped
- A pinch of crushed red pepper

Direction

Take half of the bread in the middle and make a shallow boat. Spread the pizza sauce in half and top with mozzarella cheese, pepperoni, black olives, red onions, peppers and red pepper.

Loosely wrap the bread in aluminum foil, place it on a campfire (or on a hot grill) and bake for 10-15 minutes until the cheese melts and the crust is cooked.

Allow to cool for about 10 minutes until sliced.

Grilled Asparagus

Material

- 2 lbs asparagus, trimmed
- 2 tbsp. Extra virgin olive oil
- Kosher salt
- Freshly ground black pepper

Direction

Heat a griddle or baking pan over high heat. Lightly sauté asparagus in oil, season with salt and pepper.
Flip occasionally and bake for 3-4 minutes until tender.

Grilled Summer Fruit Skewers

Element

- 6 sliced peaches
- 1point. Strawberries, slices
- Cut one large pineapple into a cube
- 8 skewers, soaked in water for 20 minutes

- Extra virgin olive oil for drizzle
- Kosher salt
- Baby, for drizzle

Direction

Preheat the oven to medium to high. Skewers of peach, strawberry and pineapple. Sprinkle with olive oil and season with salt.

From time to time, turn it over and bake for 10-12 minutes until the fruit is tender and slightly charred.
Sprinkle with honey.

Hot Shot Grilled Salmon

Material

- 1c. Sriracha
- Juice of 2 lemons
- 1/4c. Honey
- 46 ounces. Salmon fillet with skin
- Fresh chopped chives for garnish

Direction

Make marinade: In a large bowl, mix Sriracha, lemon juice and honey together in a whisk. Reserve 1/2 cup marinade for salmon discipline after grilling.

Add salmon to a large zip lock bag or baking dish and pour into the marinade. Marinated in the fridge for 3 hours or overnight.

Grate the oil, add the salmon, marinade and bake for 5 minutes on each side until cooked.

Season with the reserved marinade and decorate the chives.

S'mores Cinnamon Rolls

Element

- 1 refractory cinnamon roll
- 1C. Marshmallow fluff
- 1 / 2c. Small semi-circular chocolate chips
- 1C. Chocolate chips sold weekly
- 1C. Mini marshmallow
- 1 / 4c. Graham crackers

Direction

Preheat the oven to 350 degrees and line the large baking sheet with parchment paper.

Open each cinnamon roll and do it one by one. Spread marshmallow fluff on the dough and sprinkle with chocolate chips. Roll the cinnamon rolls and place them on the baking tray. Bake according to the package instructions until golden and fully cooked. Remove from the oven, set the oven and bake.

Sprinkle melted chocolate on each cinnamon roll and sprinkle with mini marshmallows. Boil for 1-2 minutes until the marshmallows start to turn brown on top. Sprinkle with melted chocolate and sprinkle with graham crackers.

Grilled Pork Chops

Material

- 1/4c. Honey
- 1/2c. Low salt soy sauce
- 2 cloves minced garlic
- Red chili
- 4 boneless pork ribs

Direction

Add pork chops, cover, and refrigerate for at least 30 minutes or up to 2 hours. Add pork chops, cover, and refrigerate for at least 30 minutes or up to 2 hours.

Preheat grill to medium to high and bake for 8 minutes on each side until golden brown. Please rest for 5 minutes before serving.

Sausage and Peppers Foil Pack

Element

- 8 Italian sausage links
- 4 thinly sliced peppers
- 2 onions, sliced
- 1/4c. Extra virgin olive oil, split
- Kosher salt

- Freshly ground black pepper
- Fresh parsley chopped for garnish

Direction

High baking temperature. Cut 4 pieces of foil about 12 inches long.

Bake the sausages for 3 minutes on each side until browned, then divide into foil. Sprinkle 1 tablespoon of olive oil on top of pepper and onions, and season with salt and pepper.

Fold the foil packet diagonally over the mixture of sausage and pepper to completely cover the food. Round the top and bottom edges to seal.

Bake for 13 to 15 minutes until the peppers and onions are tender and the sausages are completely cooked.
Decorate with parsley and serve.

Grilled Watermelon

Material

- 1 lemon juice and skin
- 1/4c. Honey
- 1 tbsp. Olive oil
- 1 small watermelon, cut into 1-inch-thick pieces
- Fresh mint leaves, to serve
- Sea salt flakes, for serving

Direction

In a medium bowl, whisk together the lemon juice, zest, honey, and olive oil with a whisk.

Beat the lemon juice mixture all over the watermelon and place on the griddle. Heat on one side for about 2 minutes until browned and fruit is slightly tender.

Sprinkle with mint and sea salt.

Chicken Fajitas

Element

- 1 / 2c. Plus 1 tbsp. Extra virgin olive oil
- 1 / 4c. Lime juice, from about 3 lemons
- 2 teaspoons. cumin
- 1/2 teaspoon MSG. Crushed red pepper
- 1 pound without skin chicken breast without bones

- Kosher salt
- Freshly ground black pepper
- 2 thinly sliced peppers
- 1 onion, sliced
- Tortilla to serve

Direction

In a large bowl, mix 1/2 cup of oil, lemon juice, cumin and red pepper. Season the chicken with salt and pepper, put it in a bowl and place it on top. Marinated in the refrigerator for 30 minutes to 2 hours.

When ready, heat the remaining 1 tablespoon of oil in a large saucepan over medium heat. Add chicken and cook in 8 minutes on each side until golden. Leave it for 10 minutes and then chop it into small pieces.

Put the peppers and onions in a pan and cook for 5 minutes until tender. Add chicken and stir until mixed. Serve with corn bread.

Goulash

Material

- 2 tbsp. Extra virgin olive oil
- 1 minced purple onion
- 2 cloves minced garlic
- 1 pound minced beef
- Kosher salt

- Freshly ground black pepper
- 1 tbsp. Ketchup
- 1 1/4c. Low sodium beef broth
- 1 (15 oz) canned tomato sauce
- 1 (15 ounce) tomato can be diced
- 1 teaspoon Italian seasoning
- 1 teaspoon chili powder
- 1 1/2c. Macroni elbow, uncooked
- 1 C. Chopped Cheddar
- Chopped parsley for garnish

Direction

Add onion and simmer for about 5 minutes until soft. Add garlic and simmer for about 1 minute until fragrant.

Add the minced beef and simmer for about 6 minutes until the pink color disappears. Drain the fat and return to the pan. Adjust to taste with salt and pepper.

Add the ketchup, stir and coat, then pour in the soup, ketchup, and diced tomatoes. Season with Italian seasoning and paprika, toss well with pasta.

Simmer for about 15 minutes, stirring occasionally, until pasta is tender.

Add cheese, stir and remove from heat.

Garnish with parsley before serving.

Cheesy Taco Skillet

Material

- 1 tbsp. Vegetable oil
- 1 red bell pepper, chopped
- 1/4c. Sliced scallions, for garnish
- 2 cloves minced garlic
- 1 tbsp. Chili powder

- 1 tbsp. Dill grinds
- Kosher salt
- 1 pound minced beef
- 115 ounces. You can diced tomatoes
- 1 C. Black beans
- 1 tbsp. Spicy sauce
- 1 C. Chopped Jack Monterey
- 1 C. Chopped Cheddar

Direction

Heat oil in a large skillet over medium to high heat. Add chili and onion and simmer for 5 minutes until tender. Add garlic and simmer for 1 minute until fragrant. Add paprika and cumin, stir until mixed and season with salt.

Add minced beef and simmer for at least 5 minutes until pink disappears.

Add the diced tomatoes and black beans and stir until well combined.

Add hot sauce, Monterey Jack and cheddar cheese and stir. Cover and melt for 2 minutes, then serve with onions.

Grilled Steak Skewers with Chimichurri

Element

- 1 / 3c. Clean basil
- 1 / 3c. Fresh coriander
- 1 / 3c. Beautiful parsley
- 1 tablespoon. Red wine vinegar
- 1/2 lemon juice
- 1 piece of chopped garlic

- 1 chopped purple onion
- 1/2 teaspoon MSG. Crushed red pepper
- 1 / 2c. Extra virgin olive oil, split
- Kosher salt
- Freshly ground black pepper
- Cut 1 purple onion into 1/2 "
- 1 red pepper, cut into 1/2 inch
- 1 orange chili, cut into 1/2 inch
- 1 yellow pepper, cut into 1/2 inch
- 1 1/2 lbs tenderloin steak, remove fat and cut into 11/2 inch pieces

Direction

Soak 12 wooden skewers in water for 10 minutes.

In a blender or food processor, mix basil, silanetro, parsley, vinegar, lemon juice, garlic, charlotte, crushed red pepper and 2 tablespoons of olive oil. With the engine running, add ¼ cup of olive oil until smooth and season with salt and pepper.
Pass onions, pepper and roasted meat through a soaked skewer (use 2 skewers for each kebab to harden). Arrange the skewers on a plate and add salt and pepper to taste.

Sprinkle the remaining 2 tablespoons of olive oil and sprinkle on a skewer to coat evenly.

Grill the skewers over high heat for 10-12 minutes and burn all sides every few minutes. If the internal temperature of the steak is medium rare (160 °), bake until it reaches 145 °.

Let's sit for 5 minutes.

Skewer with chimichurri and couscous.

Party Shrimp Boil

Material

- 1 1/2 lbs large shrimp, peeled and dried
- 2 cloves of minced garlic
- 2 thinly sliced uncoated sausages
- Two-eared corn, cut into four sides.
- 1 pound red happy potatoes cut into 1-inch pieces
- 2 tbsp. Extra virgin olive oil

- 3 teaspoons. Old Bay Seasoning, cup
- 1 thinly sliced lemon
- 4 tbsp. Butter
- Kosher salt
- Freshly ground black pepper
- 2 tbsp. Parsley leaves, chopped, halved

Direction

Heat the grill over medium to high heat.

Place the potatoes in a medium saucepan, cover with water and season with salt. Bring water to a boil and simmer until potatoes are tender.

Meanwhile, mix shrimp, olive oil, garlic, and 2 teaspoons in a medium bowl. Old bay and 1 tbsp. parsley. Toss shrimp until they coat evenly. Marinate for 15 minutes.

In another medium bowl, mix corn, cooked potatoes, melted butter, and 1 teaspoon MSG. Old bay and 1 tbsp. parsley. Place shrimp, lemon, potato, sausage, and corn on a metal skewer (or a wooden skewer, soak for 20 minutes). Grill the skewers until the shrimp is milky white and the lemons are scorched on the edges.

Flip once in the middle for a total of about 4 to 5 minutes.

Chicken and Black Bean Nachos

Material

- 3 1/2 c. Shredded rotisserie chicken
- 1 C. Red enchilada sauce
- 1/2 chopped onion
- 1 C. Fresh corn kernels (from two-grain corn)
- 1 (15 ounces) canned black beans, rinsed

- 12 oz (about 3 cups) pepper cheese, split
- Kosher salt and freshly ground black pepper
- 8 oz tortilla chips
- Fresh coriander and lemon wedges to serve

Direction

Set the grill to indirect cooking and cook over medium heat. Place chicken, enchilada sauce, onion, corn, beans, and 8 ounces cheese in a bowl. Adjust to taste with salt and pepper.

Tear off 6 12 inch square aluminum foil. Place one-sixth of the fries, chicken mixture, and rest of the cheese on one end of the foil, leaving a 3-inch border.

Fold the foil over the pad to create a wrap and fold the edges. Seal. Repeat with remaining foil, fries, chicken and cheese mixture.

Bake package by indirect heating for 6-10 minutes until cheese is melted and chicken is warm. Transfer the package to a plate and carefully open it. Order coriander and serve with lemon.

Skillet Spinach-Artichoke Dip

Element

- Canola oil for grill
- 1 package (8 ounces) cream cheese, room temperature
- 1 / 2c. sour cream
- 2 oz grated parmesan cheese (1/2 cup)

- 1 teaspoon. Lemon zest and 3 tablespoons lime juice
- 1 piece of garlic, squeezed
- Kosher salt and freshly ground black pepper
- 1 (14 ounces) can be artichoke, drainer, chopped
- 1 package (10 ounces) Frozen spinach leaves, thaw, squeeze and dry
- 1 loaf of sliced country bread
- 3 tbsp, olive oil

Direction

Set the grill to direct and indirect cooking and moderate heat. When it gets hot, clean it and lightly grease it with canola oil.

Mix cream cheese, sour cream, 1/4 cup parmesan cheese, lemon zest and juice, and garlic in a bowl. Adjust the taste with salt and pepper.

Add artichokes and spinach. Transfer to a 9 inch cast iron skillet. Place the remaining 1/4 cup of Parmesan cheese. Cover with aluminum foil.

Heat the pan over indirect heat, cover and heat for 10 minutes. Remove the foil, rotate the pan and keep the indirect heat. Cook for 18-20 minutes without a lid until foaming and golden. Remove from the grill.

Sprinkle the bread with olive oil. Bake on an open flame, turn occasionally and bake for 20-30 seconds until crispy.

Please add a dip with.

Tofu, Tomato, and Zucchini Kebabs

Material

- For canola oil, grill
- 3 tbsp. Fresh lemonade
- 2 tbsp. Olive oil
- 2 teaspoons fresh thyme

- 1 (14 ounce) package carbide tofu, squeeze excess juice and cut into 1-inch cubes
- 1 point cherry tomato
- 4 small zucchini, halved lengthwise and cut into 1-inch pieces
- Kosher salt and freshly ground black pepper

Direction

Set the grill to direct cooking and the temperature to medium to high. When the oil is hot, scrape it clean and lightly with canola oil. Place the lemon juice, olive oil, and thyme in a bowl.

Add the tofu, tomatoes, and zucchini and top with a layer of flour. Adjust to taste with salt and pepper. Stick skewers.

Bake for 6-8 minutes, flipping occasionally until vegetables are charred and tender.

Beer-Braised Chicken

Element

- 3 tbsp. Sauce from a can of Adobo Chipotle
- 1 tablespoon. Hot sauce (Cholula, etc.)
- 3 pieces of garlic, chopped
- 2 teaspoons. Dijon mustard
- 2 teaspoons. Chili powder

- 1 teaspoon. Spoon is the earth
- Kosher salt
- Freshly ground black pepper
- 4 pounds boneless, skinless chicken thigh
- 2 tablespoons. Canola oil, cheerleader
- 1 bottle of Mexican dark beer (12 ounces) (Modelo Negra, etc.)
- Jalapeno Ranch Choleslow, tortillas, sliced radishes, coriander, sliced pickled jalapenos, shredded carrots, lemons

Direction

Put adobo sauce, hot sauce, garlic, mustard, paprika, cumin, a teaspoon of salt and pepper in each zip top bag. Add chicken, seal the bag and transfer to a coat. Refrigerate for at least 4 hours or up to 12 hours.

Preheat the oven to 350 ° F. Heat a tablespoon of oil in a large Dutch oven over medium to high heat. Cook chicken in batches (add oil as needed) and wait 3-4 minutes on each side until browned. Delete the batch to disk.
Return all chicken to the Dutch oven and slowly add the beer. Boil for 4-6 minutes until slightly reduced. Cover and bake for 40-45 minutes until the chicken is very tender.

Remove the chicken and chop it into small pieces with two forks. Boil the cooking liquid over medium to high heat for 4 to 6 minutes until it becomes a little thicker. Add chicken and toss and coat. Adjust the taste with salt and pepper.

Served with jalapeno lunch coleslaw, tortillas, sliced radishes, coriander, pickled peppers, carrots and passion fruit.

Seared Sausage with Cabbage

Material

- 1 tbsp. Olive oil
- 6 small sweet salami (about 1 1/2 pounds total)
- 2 pink apples, half
- 1/2 sliced purple onion

- Cut into 1/2 slice red cabbage, 1/2 inch thick
- Kosher salt
- Freshly ground black pepper
- 1 C. Fresh cider
- 2 tbsp. Fresh Apple Cider Vinegar

Direction

1. Heat oil in a large cast iron skillet over medium to high heat. Add sausage and cook for 6-8 minutes until golden, turning occasionally. Switch to disk.

2. Lower the heat to medium heat and then add the sliced apples. Sprinkle onions and cabbage around the apples.

Adjust to taste with salt and pepper. Cook apples for 3-4 minutes, stirring occasionally until apples are golden brown.

3. Turn the apple upside down. Place the sausages back in the frying pan and sandwich them between the vegetables. Add apple cider and vinegar.

Toss, turn, and rotate the sausage occasionally for 18-20 minutes until the sausage is fully cooked and the apples are tender.

Grilled Corn with Red Pepper Jelly Glaze

Element

- Canola oil
- 4 corn ears
- 1/4c. Red pepper jelly
- 1 teaspoon. Rice wine vinegar
- 1 green onion, sliced

Direction

Set the grill to an open flame and set it to medium to high heat. When it gets hot, clean it and lightly grease it with canola oil. Bake for 6 to 8 minutes until browned, turning the finely chopped cob from time to time.

Put red pepper jelly and rice wine vinegar in a bowl and mix with a whisk until smooth. Brush the cob and sprinkle with thinly sliced green onions.

Marinated Chicken and Onion Kebabs

Material

- 1/2c. pure yoghurt
- 2% ingredients are yoghurt
- 2 cloves of minced garlic
- 1 tbsp. Grated ginger

- 1 teaspoon garam masala
- 1 teaspoon turmeric powder
- 2 tbsp lemon zest and 2 tbsp lemon juice
- Kosher salt and freshly ground black pepper
- 1 1/2 lb boneless, skinless chicken breasts, cut into 1/2 inch pieces
- For canola oil, grill
- Cut a medium purple onion into 1-inch wedges and halve it horizontally.
- 4 flatbreads or nan
- Cucumber and coriander yogurt sauce

Direction

Place yogurt, garlic, ginger, garam masala, turmeric, lemon zest, juice, 1/2 teaspoon salt and pepper in a bowl. Add chicken and mix. Marinate for 15 minutes.

Heat the grill over medium heat. When it's hot, make a clean and lightly oiled griddle. Skewer chicken and onions on 6 large skewers. Cook occasionally for 8-10 minutes until chicken is fully cooked and onion is tender. Bake flatbreads on one side for about 1 minute until lightly toasted.

Serve grilled meats and flatbreads with cucumber and coriander yogurt sauce.

Blackberry-Glazed Chicken

Element

- 1 package (6 ounces) raspberries
- 1 / 4c. Country
- 2 tablespoons. White vinegar
- 1 tablespoon. City

- 2 tablespoons. Cold butter
- 1 tablespoon. Whole mustard seed
- 4 chicken thighs
- 4 bee-shaped nuclear processes
- Kosher salt and peppercorn
- Fresh flat leaf parsley

Direction

Moderate baking temperature. Put blackberries, water, white wine vinegar and sugar in a small saucepan. Boil for 18-20 minutes, occasionally with puree, until 2 tablespoons of liquid. Add butter and whole grain mustard and stir.

Transfer half of the yeast to a bowl. Reserved. Meanwhile, tap the chicken thighs to dry the thighs. Season with kosher salt and black pepper. Bake, skin up, cover and 15 minutes.

Open the lid, spread the glaze a little and bake, turn it over occasionally and bake for 10-12 minutes. Sprinkle with fresh parsley and add the rest of the yeast.

Chicken and Sweet Potato Kebabs

Material

- For canola oil, grill
- 1 teaspoon lemon zest and 1/3 cup lemon juice
- 1 tbsp. Olive oil

- 1 tbsp. Pure Maple Syrup
- 1 lb boneless, skinless chicken thighs, chopped and cut into 1-inch pieces
- Cut 2 sweet potatoes into 3/4 inch
- Kosher salt and freshly ground black pepper

Direction

Set the grill to direct cooking and cook over medium heat. When the oil is hot, scrape the oil clean and lightly with canola oil. Place lemon zest and juice, olive oil, and maple syrup in a bowl and mix with a whisk.

Transfer half to a small bowl and set aside for discipline. Add the chicken and sweet potatoes to the rest of the marinade and cover with a coat. Leave it on for 5 minutes.

Chicken skewers and sweet potato. Discard the sauce. Season chicken with salt and pepper. Bake, cover, flip occasionally, brush twice with marinade and bake for 10-15 minutes until chicken is fully cooked.

Apple Seed Oatmeal

Element

- 2 cups of water
- A pinch of salt
- 1 cup of rolled oats
- 1 medium-sized apple, diced into 1/2 cube
- 1 teaspoon of ground cinnamon

- 1 teaspoon nutmeg
- 1/4 teaspoon ground cloves
- 1/4 teaspoon all
- 2 tablespoons of hemp, flaxseed, or chia seeds (using an even blend of hemp and chia seeds)
- 2 tablespoons of maple syrup

Guide

Add water and salt to the saucepan and bring to a boil.

Add the oats and simmer for about 10 minutes or with occasional stirring until the oats are tender. After half the cooking time, add applesauce, seasonings and maple syrup.

Brats with Peppers and Onions

Element

- 2 tablespoons of olive oil
- Cut one yellow onion in half
- 1 red bell pepper, sow seeds, slice vertically
- 1 Pobrano Pepper, seeded and sliced vertically
- 1 teaspoon salt

- 1 pound bratwurst
- Serve sandwich rolls or cakes and mustard

Guide

Heat a cast iron skillet over medium heat on a campfire (or camping stove). Add the oil, then the onions, peppers and salt. Boil for a few minutes until tender, then add semolina, stuff in vegetables and bring to contact with the pan.

Spin and throw the vegetables from time to time for 15-20 minutes until the vegetables are completely cooked (internal temperature 160 ° F).

Remove from heat and separate meat and vegetables into sandwich rolls.

Enjoy with mustard!

Stove Chilaquiles

Material

- ⅓ Cup of vegetable oil
- 6 tortillas, cut to taste
- ½ purple onion, diced
- 2 cloves minced garlic

- 1 can (7oz) Elpat sauce (or 1 cup chopped jalapeno and tomato sauce)
- 1/2 teaspoon salt
- 2-4 eggs
- Optional overlays
- Coriander, avocado, diced red onion, grated cheese, slice of fresh lemon

Guide

Heat oil over high heat in a pan. When the oil is hot, add the tortillas layer by layer, fry for a few minutes until golden brown, then flip once.

Remove to paper towels to drain. Repeat with the remaining corn tortillas.

Reduce heat to medium heat. Add the red onion to the remaining oil and fry for a few minutes until soft. Add the garlic and sauté for about 30 seconds, then add the ketchup, salt, and water to the pan.

Bring to a boil over low heat, then add the fried cakes. Stir and rinse.

To cook the eggs, move the tortillas to the outside edge of the frying pan and make a well in the center. Drop the eggs into the sauce and cook to your liking.

You can coat or cover the lid to make it easier to pour the sauce.

Please enjoy with your favorite topping. fun!

Shakshuka

Material

- 1 tablespoon olive oil
- 1 red bell pepper, seeded and sliced
- 1 pobrano pepper, seeded and sliced
- 1 onion, diced
- 3 cloves of minced garlic

- 2 teaspoons chili powder
- 1 teaspoon dill
- 14 ounces diced tomatoes
- 2 eggs
- ¼ cup feta cheese
- Parsley chopped
- Salt and pepper

Guide

Put oil in a pan over medium heat. While hot, add poblano, red pepper, and onion, toss, then coat and cook for 5 minutes or until just starting to brown, stirring as needed.

Add garlic, paprika, and cumin and simmer for about 30 seconds until fragrant.

Add tomatoes and their juice. Reduce heat and simmer for 10 minutes to thicken mixture.

Crack the eggs into the sauce and separate. Cover the eggs and cook for about 5-7 minutes until the whites are firm and the yolks are at the desired consistency.

Ladle the sauce from the top as needed to encourage the dish to finish.

Seasons to taste. Serve immediately with feta cheese, chopped parsley, and unfriendly slices of bread.

Banana Coconut French Toast

Material

- Unfriendly French bread 1 pound bread, cut into 3/4" slices
- 1 very ripe banana
- 1 can coconut milk (14 ounces)

- 1 teaspoon ground cinnamon
- 1 teaspoon vanilla extract
- One teaspoon of salt
- Coconut oil
- service
- Warm maple syrup
- Fresh blueberries
- Shredded Coconut

Guide

Mash the bananas until smooth in a container large enough to hold a piece of bread or two. Add coconut milk, cinnamon, vanilla essence and salt and mix with a whisk. This dough should be as smooth as possible.

Heat a non-stick pan over medium heat.

Dip a slice of bread in the flour and soak both sides for a few seconds. After drizzling excess oil, fry in pan for about 3 minutes until one side becomes golden and crispy.

Repeat with the rest of the pan and add coconut oil to the pan as needed.

Served with syrup, fresh blueberries and shredded coconut. fun!

CHEESY GARLIC FRIES IN FOIL

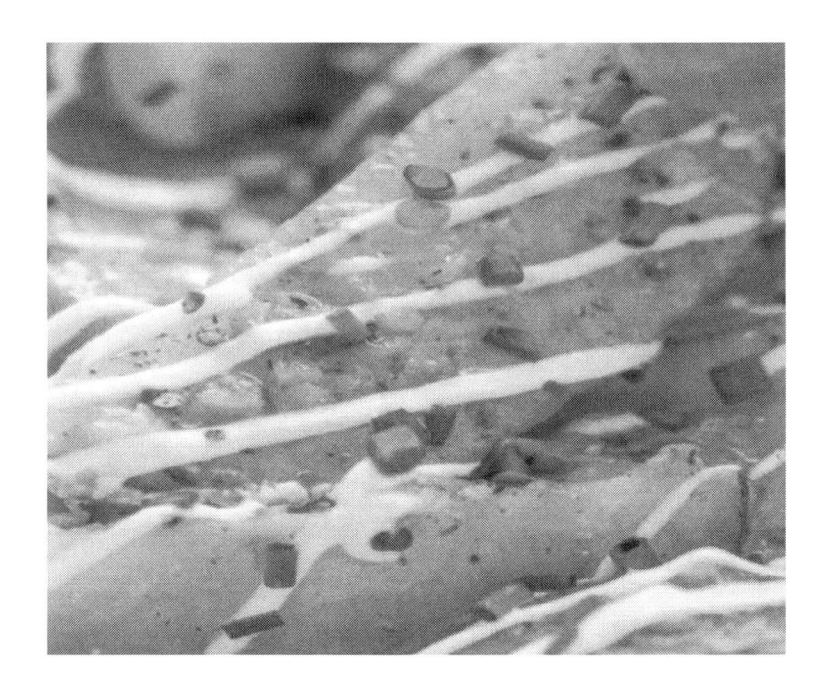

Element:

- 2 tablespoons of olive oil
- 4 pieces of chopped garlic
- More than 1/2 teaspoon of crushed red pepper, if you like

- Taste with kosher salt and freshly ground black pepper
- 1 lb of red potato, cut into 8 long pieces
- 1 cup of shredded cheddar cheese
- 2 tablespoons sour cream
- 2 tablespoons of freshly chopped chives

Direction:

Preheat the oven to 400 ° F. Line the baking sheet with foil.

In a small bowl, mix olive oil, garlic, red pepper, salt and pepper to taste.

Put the potatoes in the prepared baking tray and fold all four sides of the foil. Squeeze the olive oil mixture over the potatoes. Fold the end of the foil over the potatoes, cover it completely and seal it tightly.

Place in the oven and bake for about 30-35 minutes until tender. * Sprinkle with cheese.

Then bake for 2-3 minutes or until the cheese melts and the potato chips are crispy.

Serve immediately and decorate with sour cream and chives as needed.

Campfire Queso

Element
- 1/2 lb hot Italian sausage
- 1 / 2c. Beer (Pale ale, etc.)
- 16 oz Belvita, cut into 1 inch cubes
- 2C. Finely chopped pepper
- 1/2 (10 oz) can of Rotel tomato
- Fresh coriander, chopped and used

- Sliced jalapeno, served
- Tortilla chips to offer

Direction

In a medium or large cast iron skillet above the campfire, use a wooden spoon to golden the sausages and bake for 5 minutes until the pink color disappears. Pour the beer on top and deglaze the pot.

Shorten by 3 minutes, add velvita, pepper and hotel, and stir until the mixture is thick.

Decorate with coriander and jalapeno peppers before serving with french fries.

Chicken Pasta Salad

Material

For Salad
- 1 pound fusilli pasta
- 2 boneless and skinless chicken breasts (about 1 pound)
- 1 teaspoon garlic powder
- Kosher salt
- Freshly ground black pepper

- 1 tbsp. Extra virgin olive oil
- 4 pieces of bacon, cooked and mashed
- 2 C. Cut a grape tomato in half
- 2 C. Spinach, pack
- 1/2c. Crushed Feta Cheese
- 1/4 purple onion, sliced
- 2 tbsp. Dill chopped

Wear clothes
- 1/4c. Extra virgin olive oil
- 3 tbsp. Red wine vinegar
- 1/2 teaspoon Italian seasoning
- 1 minced garlic
- 1 tbsp. Dijon mustard
- Kosher salt
- Freshly ground black pepper

Direction

Place in a large pot of boiling salted water, follow package directions and cook until mushrooms are fully cooked. Drain and transfer to a large bowl.

Season chicken breasts with garlic powder, salt and pepper. Heat oil over medium heat in a large saucepan. Cook chicken until golden and cook for 8 minutes on both sides. Let it rest for 10 minutes, then cut into 1 inch.

Otherwise, make the sauce. In a medium bowl, mix oil, vinegar, Italian seasoning, garlic, and mustard with a whisk. Adjust to taste with salt and pepper.

Combine all remaining ingredients in a large pasta bowl and mix. Pour dressing over salad, stir until coated, and serve on a plate.

Breakfast Foil Packs

Element
- 6 big eggs
- 1/2c. milk
- Kosher salt
- Freshly ground black pepper
- 1 pound frozen hash brown (thaw if frozen)
- 1C. Chopped ham
- 2C. Chopped cheddar

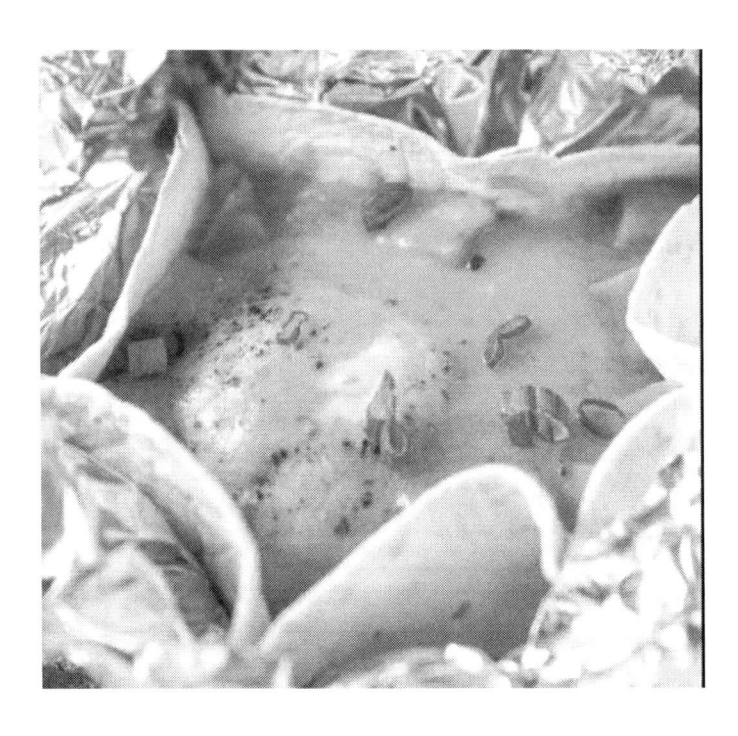

- Butter for foil
- Fresh chives chopped for garnish

Direction

Break the egg into a large plastic bag with a lid, add milk, and season with salt and pepper. Add chopped brown flour, ham and cheese.

Butter the four squares of aluminum foil and divide the mixture between the pieces of foil. Fold it tightly and seal it.

Place the packet on a campfire or grill and cook for about 10 minutes until the scrambled and chopped eggs turn light brown and crispy.

Decorate the chives and serve.

Cajun Shrimp Kebabs

Material
- 1 pound shrimp
- 2 tbsp. Olive oil
- 1 teaspoon kosher salt
- 1 teaspoon Cayenne
- 1 teaspoon chili powder
- 1 teaspoon garlic powder

- 1 teaspoon onion powder
- 1 teaspoon oregano
- 2 lemons, thinly sliced horizontally

Direction

Heat the grill over medium to high heat.

Make the Cajun seasoning mix. Combine salt, cayenne pepper, paprika, garlic powder, onion powder, and oregano in a small bowl. Use a fork to stir until the mixture is uniform.

Place shrimp in medium bowl with olive oil. Add seasoning mixture and stir until shrimp are evenly coated. Pass shrimp and limes through a metal skewer (or wooden skewers soak for 20 minutes).

Grill the skewers until the shrimp are milky white and the lemons are burnt. Flip once in the middle for a total of about 4 to 5 minutes.

Campfire Cinnamon Rolls

Element

- 1 can of refractory cinnamon rolls

Direction

Skewers of cinnamon rolls.
Bake the campfire (ideally low heat) for 15-20 minutes until golden and the center is cooked.
Sprinkle with ice and eat immediately.

Grilled Chicago Dogs

Material
- 8 sausages
- 8 hot dog sandwiches
- Bread and sourdough, slices
- 1 C. Sliced cherry tomatoes
- 1/4c. Chopped white onion
- Sweet pickle taste
- 1 C. Chopped lettuce
- Yellow mustard, to serve

Direction

Heat a griddle or grill pan over medium to high heat and grill the sausages on both sides for 2 minutes.

Sausage: Arrange slices of pickle on bread, then add sausage and place tomato, onion, bay leaf and lettuce on top. Sprinkle with mustard and serve.

Campfire Nachos

Material

- 1 tablespoon neutral flavored oil
- ½ pound tortilla chips
- 1 can hot Elpat tomato sauce (7.75 oz), or equivalent
- 1 cup shredded Mexican cheese mix

- 1 (14.5 oz) canned black beans, drained
- 1 large avocado, cubed
- 4-5 slices of onion
- A handful of fresh coriander, chopped
- 1 small lemon, cut into bite-sized pieces

Guide

Lightly oil the bottom of a large Dutch oven to prevent the nachos from sticking together.

On the first layer, spread 1/3 of the fries in a Dutch oven and top with ¼ can Elpat, ¼ can black beans, ¼ cup cheese, and some butter, green onions, and coriander. Repeat for the second layer.

For the third and final layer, use remaining 1/3 of the fries, 1/2 can of Elpat, 1/2 can of black beans, 1/2 cup of cheese, remaining butter, onion, and veggies odor.

Cover the Dutch oven and place on a metal griddle above the campfire for about 10 minutes until the cheese is melted. Serve with a slice of lemon.

Tzatziki Chicken Skewers

Element

- 2 tablespoons of olive oil
- 1 lemon, juice
- 1 tablespoon of dried oregano leaves
- 1/2 teaspoon garlic powder
- Salt spoon

- 4 boneless chicken thighs, no skin, cut into 1 inch
- 1 small zucchini, cut into 1/4 inch
- 1 chopped purple onion
- 14 cherry tomatoes
- Prepare ½ cup and buy Tzatziki at the store or a recipe like this
- Zajiki sauce
- Greek yogurt ½ cup
- ¼ cucumber, sowed and finely chopped
- 1 teaspoon chopped fresh mint
- 2 pieces of garlic, chopped
- Salt spoon

Guide

Mix olive oil, lemon juice, oregano, garlic powder and 1/2 teaspoon salt in a bowl. Add chicken and toss and coat. Leave for 30 minutes (up to 2 hours) for marinade, stirring occasionally.

To make Tzatziki (you can make it first):
Use a towel to remove excess water from the chopped cucumber. Put cucumbers, Greek yogurt, mint, garlic and salt in a small bowl and mix well.

If made in advance, cover it and store it in the refrigerator. Prepare a grill or campfire for the grill.

Skewer chicken and vegetables and skewer.
When you're done, place the skewers on the grill and the grill, turn it over every few minutes, and cook evenly on all sides. Chicken should be baked for 3-5 minutes on each side and vegetables for about 10-12 minutes.

Remove the skewers. Add tzatziki to soak. interesting!

Chickpea Curry

Material

- 1 tablespoon oil or buffalo milk butter
- 1 onion, diced
- 1 tablespoon Garam masala
- 1 teaspoon cinnamon
- 1 teaspoon ground ginger
- 1 teaspoon turmeric powder

- ¼ cayenne pepper, optional, omitted due to mild heat
- 1 teaspoon salt
- 2 tablespoons ketchup
- 1 can coconut milk (14 ounces)
- 1 (14 ounces) chickpeas, drained
- Cut 1 lemon into wedge shape
- A handful of coriander, chopped
- ¼ cup yogurt, optional, non-dairy or Greek

Guide

Heat oil or buttermilk in a saucepan over medium heat, add onion and fry until translucent, but not brown.

Add Garam masala, turmeric, ground ginger, cinnamon, and cayenne pepper and stir gently until seasonings kick in.

Add coconut milk, ketchup, and salt. Stir until the tomatoes are completely combined with the coconut milk, then add the green beans.

Cook over medium to medium heat for 10 or 15 minutes, stirring frequently until the sauce is to your taste.

In the meantime, prepare your party (see serving suggestions).

Squeeze lemon into the chickpea curry, add yogurt for $1 (optional), and add more coriander.

Dutch Oven Mac & Cheese

Element

- 2 glasses of pasta
- 2 cups of water
- 2 tablespoons butter
- Salt spoon

- 4 cups of shredded cheddar cheese
- 1-2 teaspoons of mustard
- 1/4 teaspoon garlic powder
- 5 oz bag jalapeno chip brand kettle

Guide

Prepare coal and campfire.

Place pasta, water, butter and elbow salt in a 4-quart Dutch oven. Place a cover on the bed of embers or small embers.

Place 10 to 15 coals in a Dutch oven. Cook for about 10 minutes until the pasta is tender and most (but not all) of the liquid is absorbed.

Carefully remove the Dutch oven from the campfire and set the lid aside.

Add finely chopped cheese, mustard and garlic powder, stir well and add salt as needed.

Serve in a bowl or plate and top with mashed kettle brand jalapeno fries. interesting!

Foil Wrapped Baked Sweet Potatoes and Chili

Material

- 4 medium sweet potatoes
- 1 onion, diced
- 1 tablespoon olive oil
- 15 oz can green beans, drained

- 6 ounces canned ketchup
- can of beer
- 1 teaspoon chili powder
- 1/2 tbsp dill
- 1/2 teaspoon salt
- Other optional toppings:, scallions, cheese, butter, etc.

Guide

Wrap each sweet potato in strong foil and place in the embers of a campfire. Turn them over often so they cook evenly.

While the potatoes are cooking, make the chili. Heat oil in a pan over medium heat. While still hot, add 3/4 of the diced onion (keep the rest as a topping) and fry for a few minutes until the onions are soft. Add beans, ketchup, beer (or other liquids like soup) and seasoning. Stir and mix. Boil for 15-20 minutes.

When the potatoes are soft and cooked through (about 30 minutes total, add a little or a little depending on the size), remove from the heat. Carefully open the foil package.

Slice the potatoes with a knife and place the peppers, onions, and other things you have on top. fun!

Chicken Pineapple Kabobs

Material

- For the marina:
- ¼ cup olive oil
- Coriander, chopped cup
- 1 teaspoon honey
- 2 tablespoons minced ginger, Note: Trader Joe's carries the best ginger for this

- 1 lemon, juice
- 1 teaspoon salt
- To make a skewer:
- ½ pound boneless, skinless chicken thighs are best and cut into 1-inch pieces
- 1 medium purple onion, cut into 1-inch pieces
- Season with pineapple, cut into 1-inch cubes (see note)

Guide

Place marinade ingredients in a large bowl or small bag.

Put the chicken in the seafood bowl, stir and coat. Cover or seal container and marinate for at least 1 hour or up to 24 hours. If you want to marinate for more than an hour, put it back in the cooler.

In the meantime, light a barbecue or campfire.

Skewer chicken and vegetables to make a cabob. Polish with a small amount of oil.

Bake the cabob over medium to high heat and flip occasionally to cook evenly until the chicken is completely cooked through - about 10 minutes total.

Take it out of the oven and enjoy!

Pie Pizza Pockets

Element

Pizza

- 2 cups of medium-strength flour
- Quick Rise East 1 Pack
- 2 teaspoons of salt
- 1 cup of hot water
- 2 tablespoons of olive oil

Filling

- ½ cup pizza sauce
- 1 cup of low-moisture shredded mozzarella cheese
- 1 blue bell pepper, diced
- 4 ounces of sliced black olives, drain
- Pepperoni 16 slices
- oil

Guide

Make the dough (you can make it first!): In a mixing bowl, stir the flour, yeast and salt together. Add oil and water.

Using a spoon or fork, mix the ingredients until the dough is formed. If it's too damp, add flour and knead until balls are formed. Cover and let stand up for 20 minutes. * Or use ready-made fabrics.

Divide the dough into 8 parts. Work with two pieces at a time, stretch and flatten the dough into a square of approximately 4½x4½ inches.
Oil the toaster and push the square dough into the bottom plate. Prepare the ingredients: 2 tablespoons of dressing,

followed by ¼ cup cheese, ¼ peppers, 1 ounce olive, 4 peperonis. Top with a second square of fabric. Close and lock the toaster.

Cook on a heat or charcoal stove until the crust turns golden and turn it over as needed to ensure uniform heat. The exact time depends on the strength of the campfire, but usually this only takes a couple of minutes. Check back often!

Remove from heat, carefully unlock the iron, and turn the pizza bag over.

Repeat with the rest of the material. Keep in mind that the iron will get hot when lining up the next pizza bag. Wait for the iron to cool or be very careful when reloading the iron.

Camp Chilaquiles

Element

- ⅓ cup vegetable oil
- 6 tortillas, cut to taste
- ½ purple onion, diced
- 2 cloves of minced garlic

- 1 (7oz) el Pato sauce, (or 1 cup tomato sauce and chopped jalapeño)
- ½ teaspoon salt
- 2 - 4 eggs
- Optional overlays
- cilantro, avocado, diced red onion, grated cheese, fresh lemon

Guide

Heat oil in a pan over high heat. When the oil is hot, add each layer of cake and fry for a few minutes until golden brown, flipping once. Remove and set aside on paper towels to drain. Repeat with the rest of the tortillas.

Lower the heat to medium. Add the shallots to the remaining oil and saute for a few minutes until they begin to soften. Add the garlic and sauté for about 30 seconds, then add the tomato sauce, salt and a little water to the pan. Bring to a boil, then add the fried cakes. Stirred.

To cook the eggs, move the tortillas to the outside edges of the pan to create a well in the center.

Drop the eggs into the sauce and cook to your liking - you can omelette or cover the pan to let the eggs steam in the sauce.

Serve with toppings of your choice. Exciting!

Printed in Great Britain
by Amazon